ADHD, Tics & Me!

by the same author

Can I tell you about ADHD?
A guide for friends, family and professionals
Susan Yarney
Illustrated by Chris Martin
ISBN 978 1 84905 359 4
EISBN 978 0 85700 708 7

of related interest

ADHD Is Our Superpower
The Amazing Talents and Skills of Children with ADHD
Soli Lazarus
Illustrated by Adriana Camargo
ISBN 978 1 78775 730 1
EISBN 978 1 78775 731 8

All Dogs Have ADHD
Kathy Hoopmann
ISBN 978 1 78775 660 1
EISBN 978 1 78775 661 8

The Tourettes Survival Kit
Tools for Young Adults with Tics
Tara Murphy and Damon Millar
Illustrated by Hiro Enoki
ISBN 978 1 78592 359 3
EISBN 978 1 78450 700 8

ADHD, Tics & Me!

A Story to Explain ADHD and Tic Disorders/Tourette Syndrome

Susan Ozer and Inyang Takon

Illustrated by Sophie Kennedy

Jessica Kingsley Publishers
London and Philadelphia

First published in Great Britain in 2022 by Jessica Kingsley Publishers
An Hachette Company

1

Copyright © Susan Ozer and Inyang Takon 2022
Illustrations Copyright © Sophie Kennedy 2022

A CIP catalogue record for this title is available from
the British Library and the Library of Congress

ISBN 978 1 78775 891 9
eISBN 978 1 78775 892 6

Printed and bound in the United States
by Integrated Books International

Jessica Kingsley Publishers' policy is to use papers that are natural,
renewable and recyclable products and made from wood grown
in sustainable forests. The logging and manufacturing processes
are expected to conform to the environmental regulations
of the country of origin.

Jessica Kingsley Publishers
Carmelite House
50 Victoria Embankment
London EC4Y 0DZ

www.jkp.com

Note to Parents/Carers and Teachers

The *ADHD, Tics & Me!* book is in two parts.

The first part of the book, 'Meet Jamie', is written by Dr Susan Ozer (née Yarney) and illustrates how a child with ADHD, whom we are calling Jamie, is affected by conditions like Tic disorders/Tourette syndrome.

In the second part of the book, 'Meet my Granddad and Friends', written by Drs Susan Ozer and Inyang Takon, Jamie talks about how he is encouraged by his granddad to learn more about tics, and how he and his friends with the same disorder can be helped at home and at school. Jamie's friends offer to talk about their personal experiences with tics. The descriptions of tics narrated by Jamie's friends, although fictional, are based on accounts of real children who suffer with Tic disorders.

Meet Jamie

Meet
Jamie

Hi,

My name is Jamie, and I am precisely nine and three-quarters years old. I will be ten years old soon and cannot wait to be a whole DECADE old!

I guess you are curious to know why I have written this story. I will tell you why in a bit.

Even though I am an ordinary boy like other children, I have a special condition with a very long name called Attention Deficit Hyperactivity Disorder, or ADHD for short.

The doctor told my parents I had ADHD when I was about seven years old. My granddad (who knows so much about the world) helps me to understand my ADHD by comparing it to awesome things in nature. My friends really like Granddad's way of looking at things as it helps them understand why I sometimes behave in the way I do.

Guess what? I not only have ADHD, I also have a condition called tics. Some people call it Tic disorders or Tourette syndrome.

I bet you have heard or watched programmes on TV talking about people with Tourette syndrome or tics. Most people think that having Tourette syndrome or tics means you say bad words in public but not everyone does. This book will help you understand what having ADHD and tics means for me and my friends, and how grown-ups can be of more help to kids like us.

Before I tell you more about my tics, I would like to tell you some interesting facts about myself.

Fact 1 — About me (Jamie)

I live in a house not far from my favourite park.

I go to one of the *best* schools in the world and have awesome friends. My friends stand up for me when I am teased by mean children because I have tics.

I also go to a special after school club called the Tic Club. I look forward to going to the club every week to meet my friends who also have tics (like me!).

How about you? Do you like your school and friends? Do you have any best friends and also do you go to an after school club like me? If you do, please tell me what you do at your after school club.

What do you do at your after school club?

. . . .

. . . .

. . . .

. . . .

. . . .

. . . .

. . . .

. . . .

Fact 2 – My likes

- Football
- Skateboarding
- Computer games
- Singing loudly in the shower
- Dad's banana bread (very yummy)
- Maths

Fact 3 – My dislikes

- Sitting still at assembly
- Veggies
- Mean kids
- Writing
- **MY TICS**

Fact 4 – My family

My mum and dad are cool. Mum works with computers and Dad works from home so he can look after us. Mum says she used to have an important job as a nurse looking after tiny babies before we were born.

I have a baby sister Libby who is just starting to talk. The other day I was so excited when she said my name for the first time. It sounded like 'Meymie' instead of 'Jamie'.

I have an older sister Laura who is bossy. She always tells me off for *no reason* and reminds me how much older she is even though she is *only* two years older!

Fact 5 – Pets

We have a pet parrot called Ivo. She is a very clever talking African grey. Do you know that African grey parrots are very intelligent and can live for a very long time? Some African grey parrots have been known to live for up to 40 years!

When the phone rings at home Ivo says, 'Hello, hello,' just like Mum does. Ivo also sometimes mimics some of my vocal tics. Our parrot likes me and Dad a lot but can be quite mean when Mum or Laura feed her.

Fact 6 — My friends

I have good friends at school, but the friends who go to my Tic Club are very special. I have a special bond with these friends as they also have tics like me.

Being at the Tic Club makes me very happy as I get to play and talk to children who experience similar things to me and understand me. At the Tic Club, my friends and I learn a lot about tics and how we can help ourselves and each other. We learn about the different types of tic and the feelings we have before the tics occur. We have also learnt some relaxation techniques which we can use when we feel tense.

My teacher has encouraged us to participate in the different sports clubs at school. We learnt that sports like football, tennis and netball are great activities for people with tics and Tourette syndrome.

Fact 7 – Jamie's happiest places

- First happiest place: at home playing in my bedroom

- Second happiest place: listening to Granddad talk about the world

- Third happiest place: Tic Club

- Fourth happiest place: eating my favourite dinner with my family

Fact 8 – Jamie's scariest places

- First scariest place: at school in the playground when other children tease me about my tics

- Second scariest place: when I go to new places; my tics won't stop

- Third scariest place: going to a place full of new people; this makes me anxious and makes my tics worse

- Fourth scariest place: when Mum accidentally puts the night light off and I wake up in the middle of the night!

Fact 9 – I really like facts

I am sure you know by now that I love to read and write down facts and lists!

Learning facts and writing lists makes me feel calm and helps reduce my tics.

Tell me six facts about yourself

- Fact 1 . . . .

. . . .

- Fact 2 . . . .

. . . .

- Fact 3 . . . .

. . . .

- Fact 4 . . . .

. . . .

- Fact 5 . . . .

. . . .

- Fact 6 . . . .

. . . .

Tell me about your happiest places

- First happiest place ....

....

- Second happiest place ....

....

- Third happiest place ....

....

- Fourth happiest place ....

....

Tell me about your scariest places

- First scariest place ....

....

- Second scariest place ....

....

- Third scariest place ....

....

- Fourth scariest place ....

....

Okay, enough about myself. I promised to tell you about how having tics and ADHD at the same time makes me feel and how you can help me.

Having ADHD and tics or Tourette syndrome is very tricky, and it is like having two of me. It is sometimes difficult to tell whether my fidgetiness is from having ADHD, or tics, or both!

Two Jamies

Jamie 1
Jamie + ADHD - tics or Tourette syndrome

Jamie 2
Jamie + ADHD + tics or Tourette syndrome

I have tics or Tourette syndrome because I sometimes experience movements of certain parts of my body and make strange noises. I am mostly not aware of the movements and noises I make.

The doctor said tics involving parts of my body are called motor tics, and tics causing me to make sounds or say things are called vocal or phonic tics.

The doctor told me the type of tics I have is called Tourette syndrome because I have both vocal and motor tics, which started two years ago. And my tics have been happening *every* day.

My tics

I have had tics as long as I can remember. For a long time, Mum and Dad thought my tics were just me being fidgety and making silly noises as my ADHD sometimes makes it hard for me to keep still.

I was really happy when the doctor told my parents that not all my fidgetiness was from ADHD and that there was a 'Jamie 2' (Jamie + ADHD + tics or Tourette syndrome).

Before then, everyone thought that 'Jamie 1' (Jamie + ADHD - tics or Tourette syndrome) was being silly or badly behaved when I was making noises and fidgeting – but I wasn't, I was just being 'Jamie 2'!

It can really be very confusing being two people, and difficult to tell whether some of my fidgetiness and the noises I make are from my ADHD or tics.

Teachers often tell my parents I make silly noises in class. I'm completely unaware I'm making silly noises, especially when I'm concentrating very hard on schoolwork. I also sometimes make silly noises and fidget when I am bored in class and want to move on to something more interesting.

Before having a tic, I feel this strong urge to make certain noises or move a part of my body. It is almost like the relief you get when you scratch an annoying itch secretly.

Can you imagine not scratching to relieve yourself of an itch? Tics are just like that.

(With the difference being, everyone sees when you are having tics — it is like scratching an itch in public. It is difficult hiding a tic even if you tried very hard!)

HOW CAN TEACHERS HELP?

When I make noises in class, teachers can gently remind me that the noises I am making could be disturbing other children, instead of telling me off for being naughty. Teachers can also let me leave the classroom for a short time to exercise. I like to run around the playground to help me use up some of my energy. I feel relaxed after!

Teachers can make sure children with tics have access to regular sport and exercise at school. This helps reduce their tics.

Some children have hand jerks as part of their tics. This can affect their handwriting. Teachers can let children use a computer for doing their work if the tics affect the child's hand.

My motor tics

I have different types of motor tics which come and go. My tics are worse when I am talking to some teachers or someone I do not know very well.

I do not always have motor tics. The longest I have been free of motor tics is about two months. My tics appear when I least expect them. They may also appear in a part of my body for the first time.

When my motor tics happen, I have this strong urge to blink my eyes repeatedly or twitch one side of my face. Other times, I have an itchy feeling over my right shoulder and I feel the urge to shrug or twist it. When I was younger, I used to nod or shake my head repeatedly, confusing my friends and teachers.

When my motor tics happen, I become tense and my teacher usually has to give me a break so I can leave the class for exercise. Sometimes my teacher gets me into some sports clubs so I can carry out sporting activities regularly.

My vocal tics

When my vocal tics happen, I feel a strong urge to clear my throat or whistle. Whistling when it is quiet in class can be very loud!

I have made noises like a dog barking or cat meowing to the delight of my classmates.

Whilst my classmates find this funny, new teachers who don't know me *do not*. Sometimes they ask me to go and see the head teacher at lunch time, which means missing a lot of play time with friends.

Some mean kids have called me some horrible names as they do not understand why I do this. I have seen some kids copying my tics and this still upsets me a lot.

Before my tics diagnosis

A few years ago, before my diagnosis, at a very important school assembly, I suddenly had the urge to shout 'Fire!' and so I did. It caused a huge uproar with children running out of the assembly because they thought there was a real fire. I didn't mean to cause a panic, it was just my vocal tic.

I felt very embarrassed afterwards and had to apologize in front of the whole school the next day after getting a big telling off from the head teacher and my parents. Nobody believed me when I told them I could not help myself!

Now I have my diagnosis, my parents and my teachers know that I am not behaving badly and will not be too quick to call me naughty.

I still have these urges and strong feelings, but I am learning to control them better due to the help and support I have been getting at school since my diagnosis. This has helped me feel more relaxed when I am at school. I no longer get anxious about what my friends will think about what people might say when I have my tics.

My school has also let me use the computer to do most of my work. My tics used to cause me to have problems with handwriting. Having the computer to do my work has been very good. I have been able to finish my work at the same time as my friends in class.

I have felt so much better since I got my diagnosis of Tourette syndrome. It has helped me understand myself more, and I now know that having tics is very common and does not mean I am naughty.

Meet my Granddad and Friends

The 'upside-down rainbow'

I told you earlier about my granddad who knows loads about the world and has told me a lot of things to help me understand myself. Granddad told me about upside-down rainbows to help me understand how special I am.

Do you know what an upside-down rainbow is? According to Granddad, these are rare rainbows and mesmerizing when seen. Though they are called rainbows, they are not formed like ordinary rainbows. There are some awesome images of these rainbows on the internet.

Here is my drawing of an upside-down rainbow and an ordinary rainbow.

Granddad told me that upside-down rainbows are like a smile in the sky. Though they look like rainbows, they really are not rainbows. Upside-down rainbows form when sunlight catches ice particles in special clouds at the right angle, and are not formed from raindrops like ordinary rainbows. The colours of these special rainbows tend to be brighter and clearer and that is why they are so beautiful. They are the exact opposite of ordinary rainbows and look like a smile in the sky. Granddad says they bring wider smiles to people's faces compared with ordinary rainbows when they appear in the sky.

Granddad told me that just like an upside-down rainbow, people like me are very special. Despite my difficulties, I have a lot of talents which people will notice more with the right support and help. I have already told you one thing I am good at – do you remember what this was? I am also good at colouring and my dad tells me I am very good at baking cookies. I am part of the school choir and love to sing. When I am singing, I totally forget about my tics.

Getting more help and being understood means I will start feeling better about myself and bring smiles to the faces of more people.

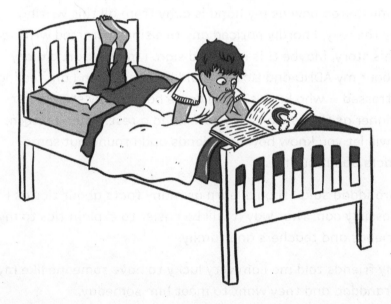

It is still difficult having ADHD and tics. When I feel stressed and sad about my tics, I look at pictures of upside-down rainbows Granddad showed me on the computer and in books. Looking at the pictures helps me feel happier, especially when I think about what my granddad told me about the rainbows.

Being my age and having a disorder can be very difficult.

I told my granddad I would love more than anything in the world to see a real upside-down rainbow one day. I know seeing one would be the happiest day of my life! I told my friends about it and we have a competition on who might spot a real upside-down rainbow!

I must stop now as my hand is achy from all this writing. By the way, I hardly noticed any tics since I started writing this story. Maybe this is a good sign. I might start a diary about my ADHD and tics. It could help me when I am feeling stressed – who knows? I will come back to my story after dinner as this will give my sore hand a rest. When I return, I will let you know how my friends and I found out some facts about our tics.

Granddad said I should learn as many facts about tics as I possibly can! That way it will be easier to explain tics to my friends and teachers and family.

My friends told me I am very lucky to have someone like my granddad and they want to meet him someday.

As my friends and me wanted to know about tics, Miss Anu, our Tic Club teacher, decided to make learning about tics fun by dividing the club into two groups. The group who could find the most facts would be the winner. One group would look for facts on tics from a computer, while the other group would find facts from a smart device called a virtual assistant or smart speaker.

Do you know what a virtual assistant or smart speaker is? Virtual assistants are like very clever robots or smart devices. They are called smart because they can do many clever things like play music, set alarms and tell the news and weather when asked. We were very excited when Dad brought home our first virtual assistant. The device is now part of our family, and especially loved by our parrot Ivo. Ivo likes to tell the virtual assistant to play Dad's favourite classical music. We always come home from school to the sound of classical music playing loudly with Ivo fast asleep!

Anyway, below are the facts our club found about tics and Tourette syndrome. My friends have agreed to write about how tics make them feel. They told me they wanted to help people understand how tics make children like us feel — but you need to read the facts we found out first!

Fact 1 — Winner, computer group

Question:
What is a tic?

Answer:
Tics are very common in children. They occur suddenly. Up to 10 out of 100 children may have tics, so this shows how common tics are. Children with tics may make sounds with their mouths or make certain movements with their eyes, face, hands, neck or other parts of their bodies. When these sounds or movements happen again and again, they are called tics. Some tics may not be noticeable to other people. Some tics may just happen for a short while and then disappear.

Fact 2 – Winner, computer group

Question:

Can people tell when someone is having a tic?

Answer:

People can tell when some children are having tics. Children with tics make repeated movements and sounds which may upset them because they know everyone can see this. Tics that occur when you move a part of your body are called motor tics. Tics that occur when you make certain sounds or say certain words are called vocal tics. It is possible to have motor and vocal tics all at once.

Fact 3 – Winner, computer group

Question:

Can you tell us more about motor and vocal tics?

Answer:

Motor tics happen when you have sudden movements of parts of your body. Examples of motor tics include eye blinking, nose twitching, arm jerking, head jerking, head nodding and eye rolling. Vocal tics include coughing, throat clearing, barking, grunting, whistling, making animal noises and snorting. Sometimes, vocal tics can involve words such as 'oh dear', 'that's right' and many others. These words are usually short and are said again and again for no reason.

Fact 4 – Winner, computer group

Question:
What is the difference between tics and
Tourette syndrome?

Answer:
Tourette syndrome is also a type of tic, but this time the
children have several motor tics and vocal tics happening
almost every day for more than one year. Tourette
syndrome does not mean the tics are more severe. The tics
in children with Tourette syndrome are the same as the
tics in children with other tics.

The difference is that some children may have only
motor tics lasting more than one year (this is called
persistent motor tics) or they may have only vocal
tics (persistent vocal tics), but if the child has the two
(motor and vocal tics) together, the type of tics they have
is called Tourette syndrome. The treatment is the same for
all types of tics.

Fact 5 – Winner, computer group

Question:

Why do some people with tics or Tourette syndrome sometimes shout out bad words?

Answer:

People used to think that children with tics say bad words, but this is not always so. Vocal tics are caused by making some sounds with the mouth. Sometimes sounds from the mouth can be real words but the child does not know they are saying these words, which they say again and again. Sometimes these words are not nice words, making people think the child is using bad words on purpose.

Children with tics or Tourette syndrome are usually not in control of these words as they tend to come out of their mouth without any warning. Sometimes children may watch television and pick up a word from the TV. They may then say this word without realizing they have said it.

Fact 6 – Winner, computer group

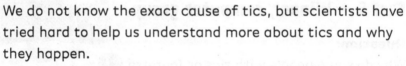

Question:
What causes tics?

Answer:
We do not know the exact cause of tics, but scientists have tried hard to help us understand more about tics and why they happen.

Our brains are like a big computer with lots of wires called neurons. Some scientists have done a lot of research on the brain and they found there are some parts of the brain that help control the movements our body makes. The neurons (wires) help deliver the messages to the parts of the brain that control these movements. Sometimes, there are things that prevent the neurons delivering the messages correctly, so some movements (tics) take place when they shouldn't.

Children usually develop tics at about age five to seven years. Tics do not tend to happen in babies and very young children, so we know that people are not born with them. Sometimes, tics may be related to our genes (these are special cells in our bodies which parents pass to their children when they are born). We know that if some parents or close family members have tics, their children may also have tics.

Tics can also be caused by some types of medication. A doctor seeing children with tics will ask their parents lots of questions to try to find out why they have tics. In many children, we may never know why their tics happen.

Fact 7 – Winner, computer group

Question:

Can tics be stopped from happening?

Answer:

Tics may be stopped or suppressed for only a short time. Children who have tics tend to report that they often have a strange feeling over the part of their body having the tic. These feelings have a special name called premonitory urges or tic alerts because they let you know you are about to have a tic.

Fact 8 – Winner, computer group

Question:

Can you tell us more about tic alerts?

Answer:

Tic alerts are feelings children with tics have before their actual tic. Many children with tics have this. They often feel uncomfortable when they are having a tic alert. It is like having an itchy feeling on your arm which you are trying hard not to scratch because you are talking to your teacher or friend. The itchy feeling will continue to bother you until you scratch your arm. Some children have described their tic alerts as a feeling of bubbling grapes inside their bodies.

Fact 9 – Winner, computer group

Question:
Are tic alerts the same as tics?

Answer:
Tic alerts are different from tics. Tic alerts are something the child feels before the actual tic happens, but tics can be seen or heard by everybody. Some children have tic alerts without knowing how to describe them. Tic alerts can help children to know how to control their tics. It is important for children to tell their parent, teacher or doctor about their tic alerts so they can get help.

Fact 10 – Winner, computer group

Question:
Will tics continue forever?

Answer:
Tics can sometimes stop suddenly and then start again with no warning. Some children will have their tics for only a short length of time, while others will have them for a year or more. Tics can sometimes stop on their own by the time the child grows up and becomes a teenager. It is generally difficult to know exactly when tics will stop.

Fact 11 — Winner, computer group

Question:

Tics sometimes seem worse at home.
Why is that?

Answer:

Tics sometimes happen more when a child is more relaxed such as when they are watching TV or doing things they like. They may happen less in school when children are busy doing their work. Please note that tics may also get worse when the child is stressed or upset.

Fact 12 — Winner, computer group

Question:

Do children with tics have other types of problem?

Answer:

It is common for children with tics to have problems other than their tics. They may sometimes feel like doing things over and over, which is called obsessive or compulsive behaviour. Children who are hyperactive and easily distracted may have a condition called Attention Deficit Hyperactivity Disorder or ADHD. Children with tics need a good check by a special doctor so they can get help quickly.

Fact 13 — Winner, computer group

Question:

When are tics worse?

Answer:

Children with tics become more stressed, and so may have more tics, when attention is drawn to their tics. It is not known why this happens, but it is important to know that drawing attention to tics only makes them worse. Some children may have more tics when they are doing something exciting, like going on a trip with friends, going to a birthday party, or going to a theme park where lots of exciting things are happening. Some children may have more tics when they are worried about going somewhere new, worried about one parent travelling, or worried about having to do something they don't like.

Children may get annoyed when trying to stop their tics from happening. They may be distressed by their tic alerts and find it hard to explain why they are feeling upset.

Fact 14 – Winner, computer group

Question:
Do children need a blood test when they
see a doctor about their tics?

Answer:
Most children with tics do not need a blood test. In a small
number of children, blood tests may be needed to check if
they have any illnesses that could have caused the tics to
occur, but this is very uncommon.

Fact 15 – Winner, computer group

Question:
Can medicines help children with tics?

Answer:
There are several useful ways of helping children with
tics, but a small number of children will still need special
medicine to help them control their tics. Special medicines
may be used to treat tics only after other things have been
tried first. If medicines do not stop the tics, doctors may
decide to stop the medicines especially if the child feels
unwell or their tics get worse.

Fact 16 – Winner, computer group

Question:

How can children with tics get help?

Answer:

Children with tics can be helped to control their tics by a special person called a therapist. Therapists help children learn how to become more aware when a tic is about to happen. The therapist teaches children some exercises they can do when they have this feeling. Children have to repeat these exercises again and again. By doing these exercises, the children learn how to control their tics. This is really helpful and makes children confident to go to places they would have been worried to go before they could control their tics. When children take control of their tics, they get less upset. The exercises the therapist does with the children can go on for a few months.

Parents and teachers can also help reduce tics by encouraging the child to do exercises that help them relax, for example breathing exercises. It is good for children to be given breaks and 'time out' when they are stressed because of their tics.

Teachers are given information on tics so they can support the children in their class who have tics. This is really helpful and makes the child feel less anxious and more confident in the class.

Fact 17 – Winner, computer group

Question:

Can tics stop children from going to
school or playing with their friends?

Answer:

Tics do not stop children doing all the nice things they are
used to doing. They can play with friends, go to parties,
and do all the fun things they like doing. Also, children do
not need to miss school because they have tics.

Fact 18 – Winner, computer group

Question:

Can tics make a child's schoolwork
worse?

Answer:

Most children with tics do not have any problems at school.
As we mentioned earlier, some children can find it hard to
concentrate on their schoolwork if they have ADHD. Some
children may also find it hard to concentrate because
of the distress they feel from their tic alerts or from the
actual tics. Tics involving the hand used for writing can
affect schoolwork. It is important for teachers to be aware
of this.

Final winner as declared by Miss Anu is the computer group!

Wow...18 facts, and all found by the group that looked up information on the computer. Even though our group looked for facts by asking the virtual assistant and lost, we had more fun than the other group and couldn't stop giggling when the virtual assistant could not make out the difference between 'tics' and 'ticks'. Ticks are bugs that bite you when they get on your skin, and their bite can be very itchy, so now you know why we laughed so much. The virtual assistant kept making mistakes any time we asked a question about tics. I now know that a virtual assistant device is good for telling facts like the time, giving answers to general facts and playing Dad's classical music but not very good at finding specific facts about tics as it kept calling tics bugs!

So, these are the facts we found out about tics and Tourette syndrome. I hope this helps you understand children like my friends and me and how you can help us. You can share my story with your friends, teachers and parents to help them learn about tics and ADHD.

I have asked my granddad to help me tie my story to a kite and watch it fly away and hopefully you will find it – wouldn't that be exciting? On your walk with your mum and dad, if you come across a big red kite with yellow zig-zag patterns, then it may have my story tied to it. After you read this, please ask your mum or dad to help you tie my story to a new kite if you can and on a windy day let your kite fly away with my story so someone else can also read my story. I hope you are able to do this so my story can reach as many people as possible.

Yours sincerely,

Jamie (Jamie 1 and Jamie 2)

How tics make my friends feel

Avi (age 9)

I remember when I started school, I used to experience some uncomfortable sensations. It happened more when I was in class but it also happened when I was with my friends. I used to feel a tickle at the back of my throat and then suddenly make a squeaky noise. The tickle sometimes happened during our lessons and the teacher would stop teaching, stare at me and say in a serious voice, 'Avi! Why are you making that noise? Can you stop being silly!' Some of the children would start laughing because I was being told off. I tried so hard to stop the noise, but each time I felt the tickle, I just couldn't stop making the same squeaky noise.

My teacher told my parents about my squeaky noise, so Mum and Dad took me to see a children's doctor – a paediatrician. I told her about the tickle sensation in my throat and mentioned it was uncomfortable and annoying. The doctor heard me making the noise in her clinic, so she told my mum and dad that I had vocal tics. 'So, what's this tickle sensation then?' I asked the doctor. She said, 'That tickle feeling is a "premonitory urge" or tic alert, as some people call it. It makes you aware that a tic is about to happen.' Hmmm! This meant I wasn't just imagining the sensations. It was such a relief to understand why I made these sounds. Now I knew I wasn't just making the noises because I wanted to. I used to be so anxious about going to school because I was worried about making these squeaky sounds. Now I knew they were vocal tics.

Shania (age 10)

My body used to suddenly feel stiff and then I would suddenly stretch out my right arm. The first time it happened, I was very surprised because I was so sure I didn't do it myself. The sudden arm stretch happened again and again.

'Oh dear, what is happening to me?!' I would ask myself.

Sometimes when I stretched out my arm, I would punch someone accidentally. My brother used to get annoyed with me when I accidentally punched him. Sometimes it happened when we sat in the car. Then he would shout, 'Shania!! You punched me again!!' He thought I was punching him on purpose! He preferred to sit in the front with Mum, and that made me so upset because I really like playing with my brother. My friends sometimes got punched accidentally too. That also made me upset as I never meant it.

I also used to feel uncomfortable when my body suddenly went stiff. I wished I could stop the arm jerking, but I couldn't. It happened so many times a day. I used to try to fold my arms to stop myself stretching out my right arm, but that was uncomfortable too.

My parents took me to see a nice doctor who said I had motor tics. He asked my parents to take me to a therapist who has taught me exercises to do when I feel my body going stiff. This has helped me control my arm jerking and I am much happier.

Josh (age 9)

'Josh! Josh! What's in your throat? Why are you clearing your throat all the time?!' my mum would call out to me with a surprised look any time she heard me clearing my throat.

This sometimes happened when we were sitting watching TV or at the dinner table. Mum would get me water to drink and then ask me to try to cough to see if something was stuck in my throat. The coughing would then start all over again a few minutes later and I would start clearing my throat again. I would try to stop clearing my throat for a short while, but this would not last long as my throat would feel so hard again, as if something was stuck in it.

My parents noticed my throat clearing sometimes increased when I was worried about going to a place I had never visited with them. It also increased when we went shopping in big stores because I do not like going to big shops because of my worry about touching germs, so I used to get stressed before we got into the shops and my throat clearing increased then.

My parents thought I had a bad sore throat, so they took me to see a doctor who looked into my throat and checked to see if I was unwell. The doctor told my parents my throat was fine but mentioned that my throat clearing and coughing again and again was not due to a sore throat but a 'vocal tic'. I had never heard of this before! I asked what having a vocal tic means. The doctor then explained what a vocal tic was to my parents.

Kizzy (age 8)

I used to get funny feelings with my tics. It felt as if there were lots of grapes in my body and it sometimes felt as if all the grapes were bubbling away in a container with a lid. The grapes then tried to bubble through the lid. This made me very uncomfortable, so I would move about to keep the container lid shut. I remember moving about so much to try to keep the grapes inside. I tried so hard, but the grapes could not stay in any more, so they did come out of the container. I remember feeling a lot better and more comfortable when it seemed as if all the grapes had come out of the container. The feeling of relief would not last long as the bubbling grapes feeling would start all over again and could go on and off all day.

Manu (age 11)

Sometimes I tap my ankle against my chair over and over again. This is what happens when I get my leg tic. It is so annoying. It stops me from concentrating on my work. I sometimes kick my friend's chair due to my tic and she gets annoyed with me. I keep having an unpleasant feeling over my ankle and then I kick my leg. The feeling keeps bothering me, bothering me, and I try to ignore the feeling, but it keeps bothering me. I get worried when the teacher asks me questions because the unpleasant feeling suddenly distracts me, and I forget the answer.

I also have ADHD, which was diagnosed two years ago. I got used to how my ADHD made me feel, but my ankle tapping feeling was different. My teacher thought I was moving about because of my ADHD, but I knew it was because of my leg tic! My ADHD medication helps me concentrate better but it doesn't stop the ankle tapping.

Tom (age 10)

I bend my neck and tuck my chin on my chest several times. Mum and Dad used to get a bit annoyed when they saw me bending my neck. Sometimes my dinner time would be longer because I would take a spoon of food and then bend my neck. I couldn't help myself.

'Tom! Tom! Stop bending your neck and eat your food,' Dad would say to me several times across the table.

'I can't stop it, Dad!' would be my reply.

I used to have an itchy feeling at the back of my neck before tucking my chin on my chest. I wished the itchy feeling would just go away so I wouldn't need to bend my neck. Sometimes the itchy feeling happened in class and at assembly. This was really awkward as other children in assembly would keep staring at me and giving me bad looks. My best friend Joe would ask me, 'Tom, why can't you just stop bending your neck?' I tried to tell Joe that I couldn't stop my neck bending, it just happened. Joe just could not understand how I wasn't in control of my neck.

Further Resources

Books on tics and Tourette syndrome

Chowdhury, U. & Robertson, M. (2006) *Why Do You Do That? A Book about Tourette Syndrome for Children and Young People*. London, UK: Jessica Kingsley Publishers.

Leicester, M. (2013) *Can I Tell You about Tourette Syndrome? A Guide for Friends, Family and Professionals*. London, UK: Jessica Kingsley Publishers.

Murphy, T. & Millar, D. (2019) *The Tourettes Survival Kit: Tools for Young Adults with Tics*. London, UK: Jessica Kingsley Publishers.

Niner, H.L. (2005) *I Can't Stop! A Story about Tourette Syndrome*. Park Ridge, IL: Albert Whitman & Company.

Peters, D.L. (2007) *Tick Talk: Living with Tourette Syndrome A 9-Year-Old Boy's Story in His Own Words*. Southampton, UK: Five Star Pubs Limited.

Books on ADHD

(For those books below published independently with an educational grant, more details can be given by contacting susan.yarney@yahoo.co.uk.)

Hoopmann, K. (2020) *All Dogs Have ADHD*. London, UK: Jessica Kingsley Publishers.

Lazarus, S. (2021) *ADHD Is Our Superpower: The Amazing Talents and Skills of Children with ADHD*. London, UK: Jessica Kingsley Publishers.

Ozer, S. (2019) *The Wide Awake Kidz Club and the Sleep Crushers: A Story about the ADHD Cool Kids Who Discovered the Importance of Sleep*. Published independently with an educational grant.

Yarney, S. (2012) *Rainbow: A Fictional Book about ADD/ADHD in Girls*. Published independently with an educational grant.

Yarney, S. (2012) *The Special Brain: A Fictional Book for Children about Understanding ADHD Neurobiology*. Published independently with an educational grant.

Yarney, S. (2013) *Can I tell you about ADHD? A Guide for Friends, Family and Professionals*. London, UK: Jessica Kingsley Publishers.

Yarney, S. (2014) *My Brother Booh Has ADHD*. London, UK: BAAF.

Yemula, C.R. (2007) *Everything a Child Needs to Know about ADHD (2nd Ed)*. Edgware, UK: ADDISS.

Useful organizations and websites

UK
ADDISS
The National Attention Deficit Disorder Information and Support Service
Website: www.addiss.co.uk

School Doctor Social Enterprise
Neurodevelopmental Services and Resource Hub for Carers, Children and Professionals
Website: www.school-doctor.com

International
ADD/ADHD Online Information
Website: www.adders.org

Blank, for your notes

Blank, for your drawings